# CRICKET DECODED

## YOUR GATEWAY TO THE PITCH

*A DETAILED CRICKET GUIDE FOR EVERYONE*

**YASH GROVER**

INDIA • SINGAPORE • MALAYSIA

ISBN 979-8-89067-939-0

# Contents

# CHAPTER 01

# Introduction

I was eagerly waiting for it. Silence emanated from the environment. What would happen in the next 2 minutes? Everyone was watching. "Yash, You can do it!", I heard a high-pitched voice way behind me. A 6-foot-tall boy was darting toward me at 15 mph. Beads of sweat poured from my jet-black hair. The scoreboard read, "6 runs off one ball to win". My face was pink, and I was praying to myself, "I got this. I can do it. I will do it". Suddenly, I saw the ball bounce and spew at me. My mind paused, "This is it. My efforts for the last ten years. The ups and downs. My pride and joy. It all comes down to this." All of a sudden, I felt my arms follow the 22 cm (8-inch) rock-hard ball with my bat. Suddenly, there were roars from the crowd. I had thwacked the ball out of the ground. The commentator shouted, "The captain – he's done it. He's done it once again". Discord broke out; people were screaming, crying, and dancing. I thought to myself, "Wow, Cricket has won again," while laughing joyfully.

Cricket. What is Cricket? This is a highly poignant question in the heads of millions worldwide. Simply said, Cricket is a sport. However, it is much, much more than that. Cricket is a way of life, often labeled a "religion" by cricket lovers. It is the real-life fantasy of a person. So popular and close to the heart, it is for millions around the globe that even a 9-year-old boy from the countryside in Bangladesh can have a deep connection to a 63-year-old *cricket tragedy in England. Cricket is the same calling that has caused shrieks across countries and tears for millions and thousands of controversies. It brings everyone together to the same game. Everyone faces the world's biggest ups and downs together. As said in the Gospel of Matthew, "You live by the sword, you die by the sword."

Personally, it has been an integral part of my childhood. There were some days when you couldn't wipe the smile off my face. For instance,

the day Shane Watson lifted the BBL cup for Sydney Thunder as a champion or the day M.S. Dhoni hit the six out of Wankhede Stadium, captaining India to a World Cup win. There were other days when you

would see me listening to sad music for hours on end to deal with the retirement of AB De Villiers, one of the greatest cricketers to have ever been born. Cricket has played a component in every aspect of my life.

There hasn't been a moment that I'm not thinking about cricket, and it's a connection to my surroundings. Dreaming about the next time I'll be able to pick up my 96 cm (32-inch) SS-branded English willow bat and smash a ball out of the park or bowl a ball so amazing it deceives everyone, and I get a prized wicket.

Cricket defines lives, mindsets, and emotions, making it one of the most beautiful events. Cricket is for the masses, for everybody. Learning about it is just as fun as watching it, playing it, and strategizing about it. The most simple yet organized and systemic games, it is truly remarkable how a sport can perfectly fit our every craving. Cricket is meant for our minds and bodies alike. Cricket is no stranger to twists and turns, high adrenaline, and nail-biting moments to keep you on the edge of your seat, crossing your fingers for what could only be an epic last-ball finish.

Join me on the adventurous, breathtaking, and spectacular journey that is cricket. Let's embark on this life-changing voyage into something that will make you so awe-inspired and blind-sided that you will go running to your nearest cricket store to start playing.

This is a warning that you might just become infatuated, making you a cricket tragic, a cricket *cricket nuffie joining myself and millions across the world into something so prodigious that it's inexpressible.

If one loves fun, they will 100% love Cricket. It is nothing but fun. Sure, it can be overwhelming at first. But only those with real drive will have the privilege to enjoy this happiness factory of a sport.

# CHAPTER 02

# History

*https://mynewsearch.net/search/?q=what%20was%20 crickeet%20initiallly%20like*

Cricket wasn't thought of yesterday or the day before that. Cricket has official beginnings dating back more than 400 years. Cricket is a highly historical sport. Rising from southeastern England, it has grown leaps and bounds. Starting as a sport made by children using hockey sticks and stones, its sole aim was for a batsman to intercept a ball going towards its goal (the wickets). It was played on a much smaller field where ball rolling was permitted. Modern-day cricket hugely differs. Today, there are close to 42 laws with hundreds of sub-parts. Cricket is played across all continents (except Antarctica) – and it is broadcast across all of them.

It was originally invented by children in the area of 'Weald', using tools found in the wild and all-natural elements as components, such as wickets, landscapes, and equipment. Furthermore, it was played in the murky woods of a dark and cold Sussex and Kent area, with it being a childhood pastime but never anything more than that.

"It is said that cricket originated in England. Since they used to raise sheep, the grass was so short that it was possible to roll a lump of wool on it which they used as a ball."

https://berkhamstedsports.com/10-fun-facts-about-cricket

In the 17th century, adults began experimenting with the game, playing it for enjoyment and later for a more competitive purpose. As kings and players in England participated, it spread to countries colonized by England, such as Australia and India. There was continued growth, with laws being revised more frequently as cricket gained more exposure and experience worldwide, impacting equipment, tools, the playing area, mindset, and many other components—a massive transformation as time progressed.

Soon enough, nations saw a way to pit their players against each other, generate a large sum of money, and engage in a challenging and fearless competition while providing tons of entertainment. One of the first-ever international series involved England traveling to Australia to play them, eventually leading to a lifelong rivalry between the two countries called 'The Ashes'.

Cricket was an escape for many places across the world, a way to cope with war, crime, and poverty by watching different nations and players battle it out, as well as by playing it wherever they saw fit, ensuring tons of fun and enjoyment while feeling excitement throughout.

Since cricket was carried by the English colonizers to various parts of the world, other countries learned how to wield bats, bowls, and fields, and master the art of cricket. Today, more than 100 countries play cricket at an international level.

https://www.icc-cricket.com/about/development

Concepts like World Cups, limited-over games, and the shortening of longer formats all began to evolve, transforming cricket into a truly diverse sport that has become an appealing concept for people of all socio-economic backgrounds, genders, and ages in all parts of the globe. This has catalyzed a significant shift to the current-day cricket, which is a cricket enriched by the riches of its history portrayed by the many centuries that preceded it.

**https://www.espncricinfo.com/player/donald-bradman-4188**

★ An Australian player named Donald Bradman, often referred to as 'The Don,' is considered to be one of, if not the greatest batsman in history. He scored 6,996 runs in 52 test match games with an astonishing average of 99.94. Not only was this the highest average ever recorded, but it remains an unbeatable record. He is regarded as a man who could place the ball wherever he wanted, making it close to impossible to dismiss him. He eventually retired in 1948 after a 20-year career.

# CHAPTER 03

# Cricket Rules

Cricket is a game that focuses on short-term goals and minor results that lead to a win, tie, draw, or loss. Its priorities are to have small, impactful moments throughout the game that can have a huge impact on the overarching result. Depending on the format and match scenario, these moments will vary, but there are often similarities in priorities. For example, getting the prized wicket of a batter in prime form early in their innings (not allowing them to score too much) is a massive moment

that can help the bowling team reduce the opposing team's runs. However, a maiden over (all dot balls) early on in a One Day International game may not be as impactful to the game's result, as there hasn't been anything significant taking place.

The game's primary objective is to score more runs than the opposing side's total. Each team contains 11 players that play throughout the match (actively and whenever required), whereas 1 (this player is called the 12th man) official substitute is put down only to the field in case of an injury, and four more replacements are allowed to field as well. Recently, a law has been implemented to enable concussion substitutes for any player who gets concussed while playing and is deemed unfit to play after a test, gets a like-to-like replacement by

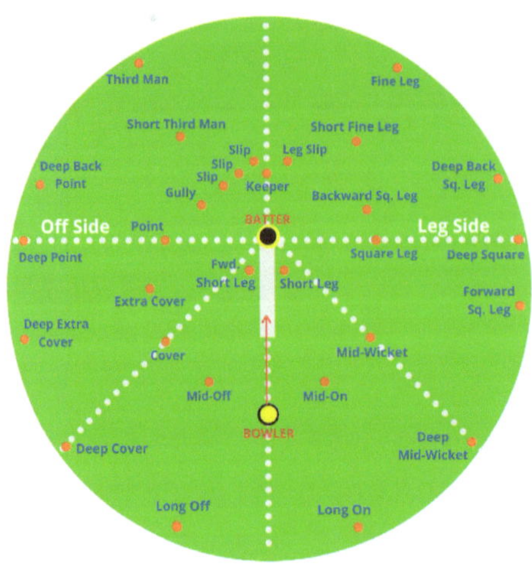


someone else in the squad (for example, a batter will replace a batter, a bowler will replace a bowler, etc.)

In certain leagues, there is an up-and-coming rule of an actual substitute (Super-Sub) who can come in and replace a player once they have completed their job, adding depth and balance to a team. Since everyone plays a very different role in Cricket focusing on other aspects of the game, is key to ensuring strength in each team's department.

Thirty minutes before the game, a coin toss takes place (or a bat flip in some tournaments like the BBL) to decide who bats first/fields first, conducted by the captains of each respective team. At this point, both teams are announced by the captains, as well as the decision to bat/ bowl based on the conditions and their effect on making it simpler or more challenging for a batter to play. For example, in the subcontinent with an even batting surface in sunny bright day conditions, it will be much easier for a batter to play scoring shots and score more. However, in the cold, dark winter of England with an uneven bouncing pitch that seams and swings unpredictably, it would aid the bowlers more, and hence they would go with that route.

Once the game starts, the batting team will send out two batters (the batting order is usually decided in advance), while the fielding team will send out nine fielders, one wicketkeeper, and one person to begin the bowling proceedings. The fielders can be strategically placed anywhere as long as they follow the rules of the format and don't interfere with the umpires or the batting surface in any way. In official cricket formats (excluding disabled, blind, or deaf cricket, or any other varying formats), the game is always played on an oval grass outfield that has its middle paved to create a pitch for batting and bowling.

In all official formats of cricket, batters always work in pairs and can't bat individually. This is because, while a batter can score runs ranging from 1 to 5, they need to run between the wickets, and this requires a partner to tap the other crease with any part of themselves to complete a legal run (otherwise, it won't count). Hence, once ten wickets fall, there is no opportunity to have two batters who are still not out, and the innings is deemed to

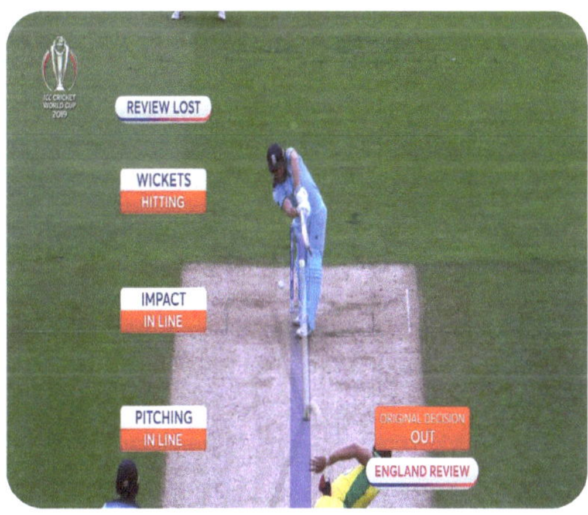


have ended when only one batter is still not out.

The goal of the batting team is to play run-scoring shots (frequency depending on the scenario/format) to score runs and avoid getting themselves or their partner out at any cost. To do this, they attempt to intercept the ball with their bat to hit it away from the wickets. The wickets consist of three wooden sticks (stumps) planted into the ground surface and two bails placed on top of them. Every time both batters successfully run to the opposite crease, they get a run added to the player and team's tally. It is crucial that both partners cross each other and reach their partner's crease moving into the opposing crease, if this doesn't happen, the run doesn't count, and it is called a short run. This can happen up to 5 times. The batters can also directly play the ball to a boundary rope. The boundary rope is a rope that marks the oval circumference of the ground. This boundary is at the edge, meaning the player has to skillfully or powerfully hit the ball to the edge of the ground, beating all fielders in the process. Four runs are awarded if the batter hits the ball to the boundary after the ball has bounced at least once. However, the most entertaining and exciting cricket play by far is the six. This can happen when the batter powers the ball out of the playing field (oval base) by lofting it over the boundary or on the edge.

The ball must clear all fielders in the air for a six and fly over the boundary. However, this can be extremely risky. If the batter mistimes

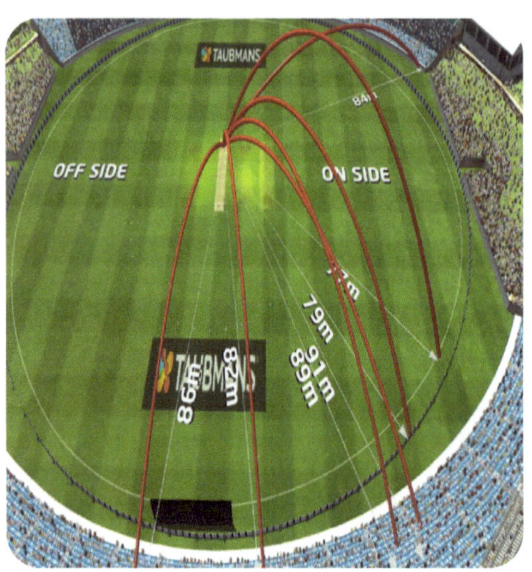


the ball while attempting to hit a six, they can end up lobbing or hitting it straight to the fielder, who can catch it and get them out. They can also end up missing it altogether in the quest for power. Both fours and sixes can happen intentionally or unintentionally. For example, it is possible that a batter can aim to block a ball but, in the process, edges the ball to the boundary behind them for a four. Also, no physical running is required to complete a four or six.

One of the fielding team's primary goals can be to get the striking or non-striking batsman out, meaning that they can't return to bat for the remainder of the game unless requested as just pure runners through one of the many ways. Another one of the fielding team's primary goals can be to restrict runs and be highly economical, meaning that the fielding team aims not to give away too many runs to the batting side. The goals vary based on the part of the game and the format of the game. The fielding team can decide on a bowling order and bowl their choice of bowler at a particular time, with the leading decision authority being the captain and vice-captain. The coach gives their input too. A bowler can't bowl two consecutive overs. They must ensure they bowl their over (6 legal deliveries) and return to bowl after at least one over is completed. A bowler can only bowl as frequently as every alternate over. This is a consistent rule in every form of cricket. However, there is a rule that varies significantly across different formats – the number of overs in the game and bowlers. Each format will have its maximum number of overs, as well as the maximum number of overs that a bowler can bowl.

For T20's (20 overs a side): Bowlers can bowl a maximum of 4 overs each – 5 bowlers

For ODI's (50 overs a side): Bowlers can bowl a maximum of 10 overs each – 5 bowlers

For Test Matches (unlimited overs – until the team gets all out): Bowlers can have an infinite number of overs – any number of bowlers.

The ball must be bowled overarm for a legal delivery without chucking or breaking any legal bowling rules. The bowler has to step behind the crease to bowl the ball within the lines of play (tramline) or be penalized with a wide-ball/illegal delivery. The bowler has to step behind the crease or be punished with a no-ball/unlawful delivery. These

illegal deliveries result in a one-run penalty to the batting side, and the ball doesn't count toward the over. The ball must bounce, be delivered as a complete toss below the waist of the batter, or be penalized with a no-ball/illegal delivery. The bowler must have some part of their foot behind the bowling crease or be penalized with a no-ball/illegal delivery. The next ball after a no-ball is a free hit in specific formats. This means the batter can't get out unless they get run out.

All of these types of wickets/dismissals (except a run-out) are only applicable if the ball is bowled completely legally; without it being a no-ball, wide, or free-hit, and the batsman is entirely ready to face the ball when the bowler releases it.

1.  Bowled out: The ball hits the batsman's wickets and knocks over the bails, either directly or after hitting an inside or outside edge from the body/bat.
2.  Caught Out: If the batsman hits the ball using the bat or any part attached to the bat like gloves into the air, or if it takes the edge and is directly caught by a fielder.
3.  Run Out: If the batsman is attempting to run to their partner's crease to complete a run, and before doing so, the ball either directly hits the stumps or a fielder/bowler hits it into the stumps.
4.  Leg Before Wicket (LBW): If the batsman's body (not the bat) intercepts the ball while going directly to the wicket. The umpire agrees  that the body of the batsman has blocked the ball from hitting the stumps. The fielding team/batting team can review this decision with certain balls, such as balls pitching outside the leg side (right side of the field for a right-handed batsman) and offside (left side of the field), which do not count for LBW at all.
5.  Stumped Out: If the batsman stands outside the crease or charges outside the crease, misses the ball, or can't hit the

ball before the wicketkeeper catches the ball and hits the stumps.

6.  Hit wicket: If the batsman hits their own wicket, either through any part of their body, bat, or equipment, they are ruled out by hit wicket.

7.  Run Out (Different Version): If the batsman hits the ball straight down the batting pitch either through bounces or in the air, the bowler gets a hand to it or touches it before it hits the partner's wickets, and the partner isn't in their crease, it is ruled run out (if the ball directly hits their partner's wickets, it is not out, and if it touches the bowler and then the stumps but the partner is in their crease, it is also not out).

8.  Handling the Ball: Blocking the ball while there is a chance of a run-out, stopping the ball with hands and throwing it, throwing the ball after intercepting it, tampering with the ball while batting with it.

9.  Hitting the Ball Twice in one play: Hitting the ball multiple times to defend your wicket by running out, slumping, or bowling.

10. Obstructing a Fielding Player: Intentionally getting in the view of a fielding player and consistently blocking them or even physically hurting them.

11. Taking too long to get to the field/Incorrect Equipment: Taking more than the allotted time to enter the field can result in a wicket being given, and wearing incorrect equipment on the field can also lead to consequences.

12. Retired Out (/Hurt): If the batsman voluntarily retires or their captain/team makes them retire due to wanting another batter to come on strike, or due to their slow strike rate, or their energy levels, and so on, they can retire out. If a player is injured, they can retire hurt, but this doesn't count as a wicket on the scoreboard; instead, the batsman can return to play. A concussion substitute can also be a reason for a concussion substitute.

All of the above wickets are credited to the bowler, except for a run-out in any form, which gives the bowler a wicket next to their name, along with the runs they have conceded, the number of maidens they have bowled, and the overs bowled.

Every time a batter gets dismissed, the next batter in the batting lineup replaces them. After ten batters are out, the team switches innings with a normal 20-minute break between innings, or a day if it's at the end of a test day, or 30 minutes if it's at the end of a test session. The team with the most runs scored after both teams have batted with as many runs as they can achieve wins. A bowler has to bowl six legal balls for it to be called an over, and the bowler has to switch and bowl from the other side while the batters switch.

T20 Cricket: 20 overs per side/innings (about 3 hours overall)

One Day Cricket: 40/50 overs per side/innings (about a day overall)

Test Match Cricket: 90 overs per day and unlimited overs per side/innings (about five days overall)

**Great bowlers and why**

- **Images**
- **Anecdotes/Fun titbits/Records**

It is played with two teams playing at once. They each take a turn batting and bowling through innings. When batting, they send out batters to go out and bat and further send batters with the fall of each wicket.. The fielding team will aim to create the best possible field that is attacking or defensive, depending on their choice within the rules while bowling; the bowlers have the best matchup with the batters to get them out or restrict them to a lesser amount of runs. They can do this by being more economical (more defensive) or trying to be more wicket-taking (attacking) There is a large sum of international teams, such as Australia, New Zealand, India, Sri Lanka, Bangladesh,

Pakistan, South Africa, England, and West Indies. At the same time, there are tons of associated nations like the Netherlands, Ireland, Uganda, and so on. The teams and games are decided based on a schedule that is created by the ICC (International Cricket Council) in collaboration with the boards of the teams playing, such as the BCCI (Board of Control for Cricket in India) for India

and CA (Cricket Australia) Australia. The teams that play each other are also decided upon the viewership of specific battles and public opinion while the money each board racks up when their team is in a game.

The game officially starts with the toss, but in reality, it begins much earlier when the players are practicing on the pitch and the ground. At the same time, TV presenters are being interviewed about the pitch conditions and their predictions based on prior forms and battles. The players' practice sessions are televised, and the stadiums fill up with spectators. Once the 30-minute timer is reached before the start of the game, a captain from each team walks out. The home captain typically tosses a coin into the air legally (properly spun) and calls 'Heads' or 'Tails' with a match referee, a TV presenter, and sometimes a child or rights activist who stands with them for a cause. Once the coin lands on one side and is completely stable, the match referee picks up the coin with the winning side and points to the winning captain. The TV presenter mentions who won the toss, and a TV representative first interviews the winning captain. They ask them about their choice of batting or bowling first and the reasons behind it, as well as any team changes for that game. Then, they move on to the second

captain and ask them about how they feel about the decision made and inquire about their team changes. There is a further conversation with both captains. After this, in international games or if a person of interest related to cricket has suffered an untimely death, the players will put on a black armband around their arms and walk out for their respective national anthems or a moment of silence.

The win or loss is usually determined by the number of runs/wickets a particular team wins by. If the team batting first scores a certain amount, which is then chased down by the team batting second in a quick fashion, or if there is a close chase where the team batting second secures a win by scoring more runs than the opposing team, then the team that batted second will have won by an "x amount of wickets." This essentially denotes the number of wickets that are still left with the team batting second when the chase is completed. An alternative way to measure this was to state the number of balls/overs left by the time the chase was completed, but this method was not preferred as it was not seen as the most effective way to show the margin of the win. In cases where a second team could chase the first team's score down on the last ball but still have all their wickets in hand, it's a bit more challenging for a team to chase a score down quickly while losing a lot of wickets, as they are more likely to adopt a cautious approach and play a slower game to avoid losing wickets and, consequently, the game.

If the team batting first sets a high score, and the team batting second pushes as hard as they can with their individual and team strategies but is still unable to score more runs, the team batting first will have won the game (by x runs). This denotes the number of runs that the teams had as a difference by the time the second team had finished their innings and got all-out (lost ten wickets), or with wickets left, lost the game because they were unable to score those runs within the allotted number of overs.

It's also possible that the team batting first sets a score that is deemed too low, and the second team loses as "anything can happen in cricket." This can either be attributed to the team batting second getting all out or not being able to score the required runs. However, it is

more probable that the team got all out, as a low score would mean that the batters of the second team can theoretically take as long as they'd like to play and chase it down, but it's definitely a possibility. It isn't always the batter's fault that they may get all out, as an incorrect strategy, mindset, playing style, and the ball's movement and conditions with exposure to a bowler can all affect this.

When rain or unexpected weather changes occur right before the start of a game, covers are placed throughout the ground, especially on the pitch. The umpires (all three), as well as the match referee, conduct inspections every 45 minutes until there is a start time scheduled half an hour from then. A proportionate number of overs are taken out from both sides' innings for the game, which can be up to 20% of the total length.

If there is an active natural disaster or a terrorist attack (such as the team bus shooting that happened in Pakistan in 2009 to the Sri Lankan team), the game is completely abandoned. The series is rescheduled accordingly based on the conditions. An abandonment can also occur if rain or any other unexpected weather changes persist until the call-off time (the time at which the game is called off if no play has occurred). Abandonment is also applied if such an issue prolongs the time period of a game after players have been called off the field following active play, and then such an event begins.

A recently introduced method for determining the result of interrupted cricket games is the DLS (Duckworth-Lewis-Stern) method. This method calculates the number of overs completed, the wickets lost, the run rate, and player awareness of the conditions, and considers the other team's wickets in hand along with the number of overs. It then shortens the target overs accordingly and provides a revised target for the chasing team or even

adjusts the target based on these factors. The need for such a method was highlighted after a disastrous event during the 1993 World Cup Semi-Final between South Africa and England. South Africa needed a realistically possible 22 runs in 13 balls when rain interrupted the match. After a ten-minute break, the target was adjusted to 22 runs off 1 ball, making it nearly impossible for South Africa to win (only achievable through extras). This incident was viewed as highly unfair to the South African team's result.

A draw is a result that is often associated with Test cricket (red ball cricket) and is not commonly seen in limited overs cricket, such as T20s or One Day games (white ball cricket). In Test cricket, which involves two teams and four innings in total, a draw occurs when the chasing team is unable to surpass the overall score of the opposing team, taking into account the chasing team's first innings (which is the game's second innings). This typically happens by the end of the scheduled 5-day match, with some flexibility for extension based on daily events. A draw is generally seen as a more positive outcome for the chasing team, as they are often trying to secure a draw and finish the game without losing all their wickets when the target is too large, unrealistic, or when they have lost too many wickets to realistically win.

In T20 cricket, which is one of the white-ball cricket formats, and in the case of an ODI World Cup Final (other ODI World Cup games typically result in a tie, with each team receiving 1 point, while semi-finals

are decided based on table standings), if both teams end up scoring the same number of runs by the end of their allocated overs or by the end of the second innings due to being all-out, a super over is played to determine the result. A super over consists of one over per side, and the objective is to score as many runs as possible and score more runs than the opposition to win the game. During this super over, the batting side can lose a maximum of one wicket. If they lose two wickets, their batting innings is concluded. Only one bowler can bowl the one over, regardless of how many extras they concede or how long it takes. The bowler and batters can be chosen from the playing eleven or a concussion substitute if applicable. If the super over ends in a tie, it is played again and repeated until one team scores more runs than the other. However, if the super over keeps getting tied until the team runs out of players, there is no conclusive way to decide the winner in this scenario. Additionally, in a super over, a player who bats cannot bowl, and vice versa.

In most One Day Cricket matches and always in Test Cricket, if both teams score the same number of runs, it is considered a tie, and each team is awarded 1 point. In a typical scenario, a win would grant 2 points to the victorious team, and the losing team would receive no points.

The duration of a cricket match varies depending on the format. In T20 cricket, the game typically lasts about 3 to 4 hours. One Day matches are scheduled for a full day, which is approximately 8 hours. Test matches are the longest, lasting for five days with each day consisting of 8 hours of play. Each over, which comprises 6 deliveries (balls), takes approximately 6 minutes to complete. This duration includes time for session breaks, innings breaks, drinks breaks, field setups, bowler changes, and advertisements.

# CHAPTER 04

# Gear

Everybody in the playing eleven of the game wears sporting tracks and a t-shirt with the team's jersey featuring sponsors. If the weather is cold, they also wear a sweater. If it's warm, they wear a cap or hat accordingly, along with sunscreen as needed. When a player is not on the field or is injured, they can change into a more comfortable team outfit provided by the sponsors. All players wear spiked shoes to grip the muddy ground surface, with pace bowlers using sharper spikes to enhance their grip when running in for a smoother performance, as it's crucial to their role. The batter wears protective equipment all over their body to shield against balls traveling at speeds of over 90 miles per hour. The first piece of equipment is an abdomen guard, which varies depending on gender but is typically worn as the initial layer. Following this, they don leg pads to protect their legs from potential injury while ensuring they remain lightweight for running. Next is the chest guard, which is optional and worn internally, along with thigh guards for both legs to prevent any harm to the ribs or thighs. After these, they wear gloves, one of the essential pieces of equipment to safeguard their hands, which are constantly in action during play. Finally, the most vital piece of equipment is the helmet, which has undergone significant improvements in recent years to prevent tragic incidents like the one involving international Australian cricketer Phil Hughes. He tragically lost his life when a bouncer hit him, and the helmet grill failed to block the ball, causing it to ricochet and push into his head, resulting in fatal injuries. Wicketkeepers also wear wicket-keeping pads to protect their legs, an optional helmet for head protection, and gloves to shield their hands in case of direct, hard impacts.

Each team has a different jersey given to them at the start of the game to play the whole match successfully and well. While playing, they are given their jersey color like

Blue for India, but these sometimes change when they play other countries with similar colors, and the away country has to change their color to another. Other than that, they are also given a rest and practice jersey. The jerseys are consistently the same in International

Cricket. Still, in IPL cricket or league cricket domestically, they change sporadically according to the owner's choices and the rules, and so on. In limited-overs cricket like T20 cricket and One Day Cricket, and even the

upcoming T10 (10 overs) there is a different jersey for each team. Still, in Test Cricket, everyone wears the same White Jersey with their sponsors as this was the original jersey from the creation of Test Cricket, and this is some way to pay homage to the same.

In the past, cricket was significantly different from the cricket we know today. The equipment was less effective, heavier, weaker, and less secure. Teams wore white jerseys for every format, including the now non-existent T20s. Day Cricket consisted of 60 overs instead of today's 50, and Test Cricket was the most common format, whereas T20s are predominant today. Players were not as physically fit as modern-day players; they maintained unhealthy diets and lacked cardiovascular and core strength. Consequently, the game was slower, and player expectations were much lower.

Cricket doesn't always demand extensive equipment; in fact, it can be played with very minimal gear, especially when a season or cricket ball isn't used. Street cricket, often referred to as gully cricket in India, is played with nothing more than a tennis ball and a bat, typically with numerous players in the vicinity. Additionally, cricket can be enjoyed in your own backyard, using the grass and a wall as makeshift wickets, following the same layout as traditional cricket.

wickets

- **Anecdotes/Fun bits**
- **Prominent names – impressive mentions**
- **Anecdotes**
- **Fun facts/tips/Records**

# CHAPTER 05

# Playing Field

Cricket, when played formally, takes place on a meticulously prepared grass-field oval, typically curated 2-3 days in advance to ensure a smooth ball roll on the grass. A 23-meter-long vertical pitch is tailored to suit the local climate, teams, and

the specific ground setup. Different atmospheric conditions offer unique advantages. For instance, in the subcontinent (countries like India, Sri Lanka, the UAE, etc.), spin bowling prevails, posing challenges for batters from other regions. The width of the ground affects the ease or difficulty of scoring boundaries, and some venues, like Lord's Stadium in England, have notably smaller sides that are frequently targeted.

Informally, it can also be played at various venues, such as the street, alleyways, football grounds, backyards, and more, with various modified rules and changes that can make it even more enjoyable (sometimes!).

cricket, particularly for fielding, include that of a wicketkeeper, who guards the wickets to prevent the ball from straying on either side of the stumps. The wicketkeeper also takes catches, executes stumpings from behind, and assists the captain and team in determining fielding placements.

Other than that, the most essential positions are the striking batsman, non-striking batsman, and bowler, all of whom play vital roles in hitting the ball, delivering the ball, and running, respectively.

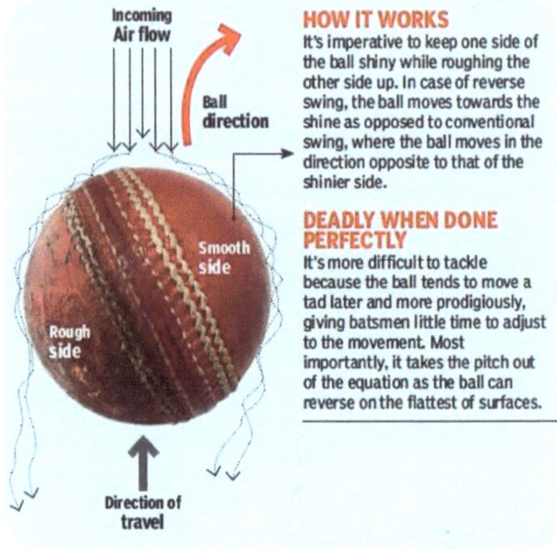


There are nine fielders strategically placed across the field based on the batter's shot selection and the type of delivery aimed to be bowled. These positions include cover, silly point, mid-off, mid-on, point, and many more, covering all parts of the oval field.

In India, a form of cricket known as "gully" cricket is common, where rules are adapted to closely resemble formal cricket with the available resources and players. In Australia, backyard cricket often involves the "six and out" rule, which applies if you hit the ball out of the yard and into neighboring properties.

In a test match or when the ball is swinging at a high velocity, an aggressive fielding strategy for the fielding team is to position fielders close to the wicket behind the wicketkeeper, known as slips. This position is ideal for catching balls that are nicked off the bat, capitalizing on the significant swing or movement in the air, or exploiting the seam and rough areas that can cause batsmen to make hasty mistakes. However, this strategy can also work against the fielding team, as the batter may find confidence in the larger gaps in the field.

- **Prominent names – impressive mentions**
- **Anecdotes**
- **Fun facts/tips/Records**

# CHAPTER 06

# The Team

In a team, there are typically around 11 players who take the field as the fielding side, with an additional player available solely for fielding, unless they are a concussion substitute. Each player has an individual role and collaborates to outperform the opposing team, with each player having a specific division of responsibilities. It is crucial for a team to achieve a

well-balanced composition, and this balance can be attained through technique, roles, experience, and form, especially when facing a particular opponent.

Some famous team nicknames include:

- South Africa: Proteas
- *New Zealand: Kiwis*
- *Australia: Aussies*

The batsman's primary role is to score as many runs as possible while safeguarding their wicket. Their approach can be as aggressive or defensive as dictated by the game format, the bowler, the type of deliveries, the match situation, the target, the stage of the innings, and the manner in which the other batter is playing.

A skilled batsman possesses the ability to adapt to various situations and batting positions, taking into account both the runs required and those already scored. They also adjust to the specific bowlers they face, considering their lengths and lines, which should align with the format, all in an effort to contribute as effectively as possible to the team's success.

Effective communication and coordination with the other batter are key aspects of their approach.

The primary objective of a bowler is to restrict the opposing team's run-scoring while maintaining economy (depending on the game format and match situation). Simultaneously, they aim to take the wickets of the opposing batters, exploiting their weaknesses and field placements, all while capitalizing on their own strengths.

Bowlers aim to deliver the right length, line, and pace tailored to the over, field placements, and the goal of deceiving the batsman. Consistency in maintaining the same line while employing tactics like swing, cross-seam deliveries, cutters, and setting up the batsman with prior research is crucial for their success.

Here are some types of deliveries used by bowlers in general:

Swing, Googly, Yorker, Wide, No ball, Bouncer

For pacers, specific delivery types include:

Off cutters, Leg cutters, Inswing, Outswing, Cross seam, Stock ball, Slower ball

For Leg Spinner bowlers:

Leg Spin, Googly, Top Spin, Arm Ball

For Off-Spinner bowlers:

Off Spin, Googly, Top Spin, Arm Ball

Some prominent names and notable mentions in the world of cricket bowling include:

Dale Steyn, James Anderson, Jasprit Bumrah, Muttiah Muralitharan, Shane Warne, Rangana Herath

The fielder aims to take catches, defend against as many runs as possible, possibly achieve run-outs, and restrict the opposing team to a minimal run total. They also play a crucial role in setting up the field required for their bowler's delivery. Before each ball, they position themselves strategically to be prepared for the impact of the ball, providing

valuable information to the wicketkeeper and captain about the game situation. In the field, there are typically 1 bowler, 1 wicketkeeper, and 9 fielders.

The wicketkeeper's responsibilities include informing the captain, assessing the batsman's hitting zones, and adjusting field placements accordingly. They may also engage in non-personal sledging to influence the batsman's mindset (optional). Additionally, wicketkeepers are tasked with taking catches, defending against edges that could result in runs, wides, and no balls, as well as stumping the batter or maintaining a forward position to distract or prevent the batter from advancing.

Each team has one wicketkeeper and a reserve wicketkeeper, positioned differently depending on the type of bowler. For spinners, they stand approximately 2 to 3 meters behind the stumps, while for pacers and medium pacers, they take a higher position behind the first slip fielder.

A skilled wicketkeeper possesses a range of abilities honed over time, often not easy to develop. They can dive in multiple directions, ensuring they receive the ball cleanly into their palms. Furthermore, they have the ability to judge the turn and bounce of the ball based on the bowler's delivery. Wicketkeepers can also assess the field and the batting style of the opposition and make decisions accordingly. These qualities are not only valuable in wicketkeeping but can also enhance their overall cricketing prowess.

Some prominent names and notable mentions among wicketkeepers include Ian Healy, Kumar Sangakkara, Mahendra Singh Dhoni, Adam Gilchrist, and many more.

- **Anecdotes/Fun bits**
- **Fielder positions on a field**
- **Qualities of good fielder**
- **Prominent names – impressive mentions**
- **Anecdotes**
- **Fun facts/tips/Records**
- **Anecdotes/Fun bits**
- **Fielder positions on a field**
- **Qualities of good fielder**
- **Prominent names – impressive mentions**
- **Anecdotes**
- **Fun facts/tips/Records**

# Captain

This topic holds personal significance for me, as I served as the captain of my school's cricket team for several years. A captain's role primarily revolves around ensuring that their players are consistently at their best. They are responsible for motivating the team, ensuring adherence to the provided strategy, and adapting to changing circumstances. If the batters are following a particular

mindset or encountering difficulties against specific bowlers, it falls to the captain to assess the bowler's necessity and make adjustments in the field placements. Managing the batting order, determining who plays at what times, and setting an example for the team are also critical aspects of the captain's role. Additionally, the captain represents the team by participating in the toss before every match.

A captain should never allow demotivation to affect them, as it can negatively impact the team's morale. They should maintain a positive attitude and lead their team exceptionally well against the opposition. While the captain's individual performance does contribute to their suitability for the role, it is not the sole determining factor. Factors such as the team's preference, the captain's experience, and their strategic thinking also play pivotal roles in the selection of a captain.

The selection of a captain often varies depending on the team's preferences. Some teams may opt for methods like flipping a coin or relying on random luck, while others might have the team members vote for the individual they believe embodies the best captaincy qualities. Alternatively, the selection committee may cast their votes and make the final decision regarding the captaincy.

Prominent captains known for their impressive leadership include Dhoni, affectionately known as "Captain Cool," Steve Waugh, recognized for his aggressive yet team-oriented approach, and Eoin Morgan, who effectively utilized his cricketing knowledge and resources to build a well-balanced team.

# CHAPTER 08

# Umpire

The role of an umpire in cricket is to make accurate decisions and ensure that the game proceeds in accordance with the rules. Umpires closely monitor the conduct of the game, and rule adherence, and are responsible for giving verdicts such as "out" or "not out." They also handle reviews referred to the third umpire, who

assesses and potentially corrects on-field decisions challenged by either the fielding team, batting team, or the umpires themselves.

Umpires play a vital role in cricket, maintaining constant involvement without actively participating in the game. They make determinations regarding the legality of each delivery, the runs scored, the field

placements, the timing, and various other aspects of the game. To protect themselves from a direct hit by the ball, umpires often carry a protective shield and may even wear a helmet. They keep track of legal deliveries using a clicker in their hands and closely observe every event, from a bowler's run-up to the

conclusion of each ball. The third umpire is also a vigilant observer. They scrutinize each delivery, its speed, and pitch and may broadcast this information. In cases of reviews initiated by players or umpires, a more technical evaluation of a decision is conducted. The third umpire examines ball tracking, snick, and any other relevant factors to ensure the accuracy of decisions.

The ICC appoints umpires based on their ranking, with progression from county and state levels. It is quite common to see former players and commentators become umpires due to their deep love for the game and desire to stay involved. A skilled umpire possesses several key qualities, including a keen sense of observation. A proficient umpire can keenly observe a bowler's foot landing, the ball's pitching, its interaction with the bat, and various other details. They should also maintain constant vigilance, listening for any relevant sounds during the game. A competent umpire remains composed even when facing immense pressure, whether it be from a critical decision, the significance of the game, or a vocal and assertive fielding team urging the umpire's judgment.

Some noteworthy umpires include Richard Illingworth, Michael Gough, Nigel Llong, Nitin Menon, and Chris Gaffney. The way an umpire signals events on the field is a unique aspect of their role.

https://www.kreedon.com/best-cricket-umpires-in-the-world/?amp

# CHAPTER 09

# Keeping Score

The scoring in cricket is the responsibility of a scorer who maintains a scoring sheet and records the score on a large scorecard for the stadium audience. This information can also be shared virtually with viewers, and it can be displayed live on television or wherever the match is being broadcast.

The winner of a cricket match is determined by the total number of runs scored by a team, with the higher total resulting in an overall victory by the end of the game. As cricket matches must have a designated result (abandoned, canceled, win, loss, tie, or draw as the options), this outcome is showcased through the final score.

The fielding team typically initiates appeals for dismissals by raising their voices enthusiastically to draw the attention of the umpire. They request the umpire to rule the batsman out when there is uncertainty about a dismissal. This often occurs in LBW (leg before wicket) dismissals, caught behind dismissals, or slip dismissals, such as edges or nicks to the wicketkeeper or slip fielders, which can be challenging to discern.

Runs in cricket are obtained by the batsmen while running or making a strike over a period of time. Team runs can also be added if a bowler bowls extras.

1 Run: This is achieved by hitting the ball away from the pitch or within the pitch, and both batsmen successfully cross to the other side of the pitch. It can also result from one wide delivery, one no ball, one leg bye, one bye, or one overthrow.

2 Runs: Hitting the ball away from the pitch or within the pitch, and both batsmen successfully cross to the other side of the pitch twice. It can also result from one wide, two leg byes, two byes, or two overthrows.

3 Runs: Hitting the ball away from the pitch or within the pitch, and both batsmen successfully crossing to the other side of the pitch thrice. Alternatively, it can result from two wides, three leg byes, three byes, or three overthrows.

4 Runs: This occurs when a shot played by the batsman hits the field's boundary but touches the ground at least once before reaching the boundary. It can also result from hitting the ball away from the pitch or within the pitch and both batsmen successfully cross to the other side of the pitch four times. Other ways to score four runs include three wides, four leg byes, four byes, or four overthrows.

5 Runs: Five runs can be obtained from five overthrows (comprising one run and four overthrows) or from a delivery that is called a wide.

6 Runs: A six is scored by playing a shot that clears the boundary of the ground without the ball touching the ground within the field of play. It can also result from six overthrows.

- **Anecdotes**
- *Images*
- *Fun facts/tips/Records*

# CHAPTER 10

# Various Formats

There are a variety of formats that exist in the game of cricket, ensuring it is wholly engaging and exciting for every kind of viewer. Test matches are the oldest and most extended format, traditionally played internationally over five days, with three umpires – two on the field and a third umpire. In a Test match, players don white jerseys, unlike the colored regular jerseys, and play 90 overs in a typical day without interruptions. These 90 overs are divided into three 30-over sessions with two breaks in between, known as lunch and tea, respectively, and a drinks break every 15 overs.

Breaks between Test matches are usually longer because they play for extended durations, and players need more time to recharge. It's important to note that there is a predetermined end time for each day's play, typically lasting 8 hours. If 90 overs aren't completed by that time, stumps are called early, and this rule applies even in the case of rain. Currently, there are tournaments such as the Test World Championship, which use a points system to determine outcomes based on wins, draws, and losses. Notably, there is no power play during Test matches.

One Day Internationals (ODIs) are known to satisfy both types of viewers: those who enjoy aggressive shots and bowling, and those who prefer a slower-paced setup. In an ODI, two teams compete by playing 50 overs each, striving to score the most runs within the allotted time and number of balls. It's essential to note that rain-affected play may involve the use of the Duckworth-Lewis-Stern (DLS) system. Each bowler can deliver a maximum of 10 overs, with a powerplay of 10 overs in the initial phase, allowing only two fielders outside the inner ring. This encourages more attacking play and offers entertainment with both runs and wickets at a slower pace compared to T20 matches.

A T20 match consists of both sides having 20 overs to compete and score the most runs. This format is often referred to as the "night out" or "party" format, as it doesn't require players to spend much time settling in and instead emphasizes short but impactful performances. With only 20 overs for all 11 players to potentially participate and a maximum of 4 overs for each bowler (with a minimum of 5 bowlers), T20 cricket is known for its high-intensity play. Moreover, there is a 6-over powerplay in the first 6 overs, allowing only 2 fielders outside the inner ring. This results in more aggressive batting, fielding, and wicket-taking, making it highly entertaining for viewers.

The IPL league is hosted primarily in India and features 10 teams representing various Indian cities. These teams have the flexibility to adapt to regular international cricket rules. The IPL works by assembling teams through an auction held before the league begins, where a budget of 80 crore rupees is allocated. Each squad can comprise a maximum of 25 players, with a minimum of 18 Indian players and a maximum of 8 foreign national players. This quota encourages the inclusion of Indian rookies in the league. Additionally, each IPL team is allowed a maximum of 4 foreign players on the field at any given time.

Gully Cricket in India, or Backyard Cricket in Australia and other countries, is a form of cricket played in unconventional environments. It aims to recreate the cricketing experience while accommodating a variable number of players. This informal version of cricket allows for extensive adaptation and modification of rules. It often involves using walls, rivers, fences, or other objects as cricketing objectives for scoring runs and taking wickets, among other creative variations.

**https://prideoflions.co.uk/get-playing/rules-positions/**

# CHAPTER 11

# Cricket Terminology

ricket comprises numerous terms that might perplex a layperson. It is a sport characterized by intricate details that you will start to appreciate from now on. Are you ready for the challenge?

**Yorker** → The Yorker is a clever delivery. It's a ball aimed at the batsman's toes, making it challenging for them to get under or reach the ball, potentially hitting the wickets. When bowled swiftly and accurately, it prevents the batsman from hitting boundaries and may even lead to their dismissal, as playing a well-executed yorker is exceedingly difficult.

**Good Length Ball** → The good length ball is a standard delivery. It is pitched at a reasonable length for the batsman to play. It is slightly fuller than a bouncer but can generate significant spin and swing. This type of delivery is frequently used in Test matches.

**Full Length Ball** → The full-length ball is designed to deceive the batsman into thinking they can play a big shot. It can induce some swing and is most commonly employed in T20s and ODIs.

**Slower Ball** → The slower ball is a change-up delivery that aims to deceive the batter by being slower than expected. The change in pace should not be drastic but rather a subtle variation.

**Boundary** → The boundary refers to the perimeter or oval circumference of the cricket ground. It is also a term used to describe a batsman hitting the ball to the boundary, resulting in a four or six. In this context, it might be used as follows: "That was a great boundary," which means "That was a great shot that reached the boundary."

**LBW (Leg Before Wicket)** → LBW occurs when the batsman uses any part of their body to block the ball from hitting the wickets. This is a method of getting a batsman out. The umpire must agree that if the batsman hadn't obstructed the ball, it would have hit the wickets. Certain criteria regarding where the ball pitches and how it impacts the batsman's body must be met for the batsman to be declared out LBW.

**Beaten** → In cricket, "beaten" doesn't imply physical harm. (If that were the case, it would be more akin to boxing than cricket.) Being beaten in cricket means that the batsman failed to make contact with the ball delivered to them. This is a common occurrence, especially in Test match cricket, where the ball tends to move more due to various factors like swing and spin. Even in other forms of cricket, facing a delivery at high speeds with possible movement can result in the batsman being beaten.

**Clicks** → This term is a playful synonym for speed. For example, a bowler might say they bowled at "90 clicks per hour," implying a speed of 90 kph or 90 mph, depending on the region.

**Bouncer (Bumper/Beamer)** → The bouncer is an aggressive delivery. It is a strategic and often tactical ball, although it can also be bowled in frustration. The aim is to bounce the ball as far away from the batsman as possible (within legal limits) and have it reach head height. This restricts the batsman's ability to play the ball comfortably, potentially leading to their dismissal or causing them to become apprehensive. A well-executed bouncer, with speeds ranging from 120 kph to 150 kph, can deceive the batsman into playing too early or making a rash shot.

**Appeal** → The appeal is a unique aspect of cricket, exclusive to the sport. It involves the fielding team making a loud plea to the umpire, requesting a decision in their favor by declaring the batsman out. Since the umpire's judgment determines whether an LBW is out or if a ball has edged (which can be difficult to discern), the fielding team exerts pressure on the umpire to rule in their favor. The appeal also signals the fielding team's belief that there is a chance of taking a wicket.

**Bails** → Bails are two wooden or, in some formats and locations, electric objects that rest on the stumps to complete the wickets. They are used to determine when the stumps are first hit, especially in time-sensitive dismissal situations. They are also examined in the event of the ball hitting the wicket, helping to confirm whether the ball made contact with the wickets.

**Dolly** → Bails are two wooden or, in some formats and locations, electric objects that rest on the stumps to complete the wickets. They are used to determine when the stumps are first hit, especially in time-sensitive dismissal situations. They are also examined in the event of the ball hitting the wicket, helping to confirm whether the ball made contact with the wickets.

**Edge (Snick/Nick)** → When the ball doesn't make contact with the center or toe end of the bat but instead brushes the

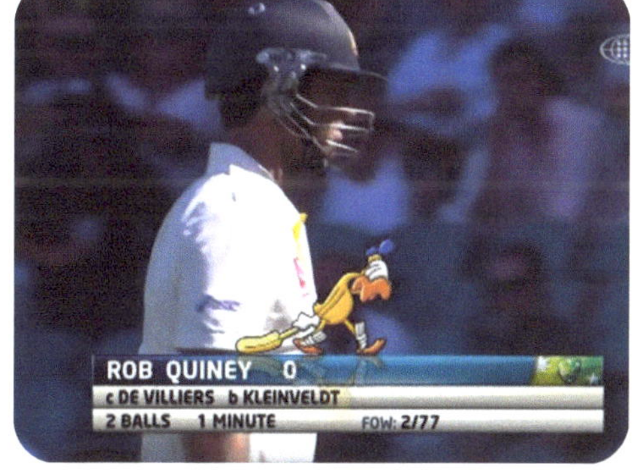

edge, there is a highly probable chance of the batsman being caught behind by the wicketkeeper or the slips. This happens because the ball has touched the bat and is heading directly back to the wicketkeeper or other fielders behind.

**Duck (Golden, Silver, Bronze, Diamond)** → A duck occurs when a batsman is dismissed without scoring any runs. There are different variations of ducks: a golden duck signifies getting out on the first ball, a silver duck means getting out on the second ball (without scoring), a bronze duck indicates getting out on the third ball (without scoring), and a diamond duck represents being dismissed without even facing a delivery.

**First Change** → The term "First Change" refers to the moment when, in a cricket match, one of the two initial bowlers is replaced by another bowler. This change typically occurs after a certain period of bowling.

**Spell** → A "spell" in cricket refers to the consecutive overs bowled by a single bowler. For example, if a bowler bowls a 5-over spell, it means they have bowled 5 overs continuously within a sequence of 10 overs.

**Rough** → In red-ball (Test match) cricket games, the "rough" refers to the deliberately roughened side of the cricket ball created by the fielding team. This roughness is achieved by not cleaning the ball, which can assist in achieving a conventional swing in the direction of the rough side unless there is a reverse swing. "Rough" can also refer to the rough or uneven part of the pitch, which can potentially produce more spin or swing if the ball lands on it. This part of the pitch is sometimes called a "crack."

**Byes** → Byes occurs when the ball doesn't make contact with any part of

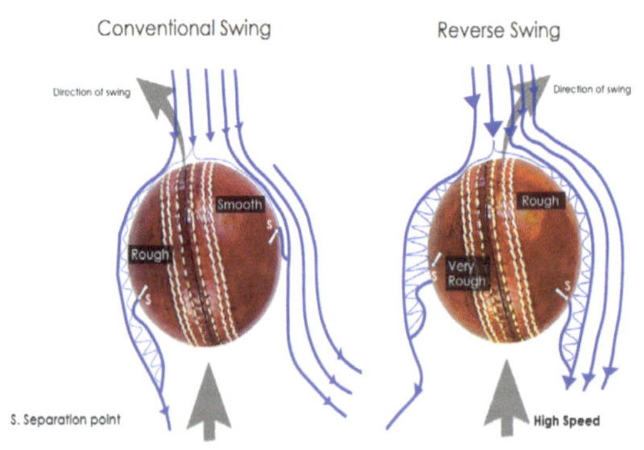

the batsman's bat or body, but the batsman still manages to run for runs, or the ball goes to the boundary. In this situation, the individual batter doesn't receive the runs, but the runs are credited to the team's total.

**Leg Byes** → Leg byes occur when the ball does not hit the batsman's bat but instead makes contact with a part of the striking batter's body, such as the leg. In this scenario, the individual batter doesn't receive the runs, but the runs are credited to the team's total.

**Shiny** → "Shiny" refers to the side of the cricket ball that is intentionally maintained by the fielding side using sweat, dew, and saliva. This side is meant to be kept shiny. It assists in helping the ball swing in the direction of the shiny side and is crucial for achieving reverse swing.

**Reverse Swing** → "Reverse swing" occurs when the cricket ball swings in the direction opposite to the shiny side. This is a phenomenon that fast bowlers use to their advantage.

**Seam** → The "seam" is the central part of the cricket ball that separates the shiny and rough sides. Fast bowlers often grip the seam while bowling, and other bowlers manipulate it to influence the ball's movement.

**Silly** → When a fielder positions themselves close to the stumps, the fielding position is often described as "silly." This term is used to indicate fielders who are very close to the batsman.

**Screamer** → A "screamer" refers to a fantastic, almost impossible catch that is successfully completed by a fielder. It's an extraordinary fielding effort.

**Jaffa** → "Jaffa" is a term used to describe an unplayable or absolutely incredible delivery bowled by a bowler. It signifies a ball that is exceptionally difficult to face.

**Maiden** → A "maiden" is a legal over in which no runs are scored by the batting team. It's an over in which the bowler successfully prevents the opposition from adding to their run total.

**Umpire** → An "umpire" in cricket is akin to a referee who makes decisions and calls during the game. There are typically three umpires in a cricket match: two on the field and a third who assists with technological reviews and decisions.

- **Anecdotes/Fun bits**
- **Fielder positions on a field**
- **Qualities of good fielder**
- **Prominent names – impressive mentions**
- **Anecdotes**
- **Fun facts/tips/Records**

## Some Extra Points

Cricket shares many similarities with other bat-and-ball sports, especially baseball. However, there are significant differences between the two. For instance, in cricket, the ball bounces, and the game is played on an oval field, among other distinctions. Cricket's objective is for a team to win based on runs, akin to points in other bat-and-ball sports. This resemblance to baseball, albeit with distinct rules and gameplay, makes cricket somewhat akin to an English version of baseball. While cricket and other sports share common goals, they achieve them in unique ways. Comparing cricket to other sports can be a valuable way to understand its nuances and differences, facilitating the application of this knowledge in the future.

Like any sport, cricket cannot be mastered without practice. Success in cricket requires the mastery of various skills such as batting strokes, strategic thinking, legal bowling techniques, as well as the ability to hold and grasp the ball effectively, among others. Since cricket encompasses a multitude of components within a single game, the key to success lies in mastering these skills, fostering innovation and creativity, and adapting to different situations. Training and practicing with various tools and competing against stronger opponents can expedite one's progress in cricket. It's worth noting that practice is crucial, as it often takes years of dedication and hard work to achieve a high level of skill in cricket. This effort can lead to significant accomplishments, such as becoming the captain of a school cricket team and consistently outperforming other schools.

Cricket is a team sport. As mentioned, cricket can't work without teams, partners, and collaboration. Hence, during cricket, everybody needs to put in their full effort and be completely involved. The only way to grow is to work with a team, make strategic decisions together, and aim to obliterate the opposition. One needs to show character and integrity; without these key components, cricket wouldn't be a 'Gentleman's Game' anymore.

Cricket is a hugely beneficial sport. It is one of the best sports for mental and physical health. You are able to exercise, work out, and improve your physical health with minimal risk to others as well as yourself. Once one gets used to the official hard cricket ball, they can play to a safe extent. There isn't much risk, meaning that you can extract the most from the sport by running, jumping, bending, using hand and arm techniques, and much more. You can feel mentally satisfied with your efforts. For example, just hitting a six can make one feel on top of the world, or getting a single wicket can do the same. Since cricket is a team game, everyone involved feels a strong sense of togetherness and community.

# CHAPTER 12

# Conclusion

You did it! Incredible. You don't know how proud I am of you. Good job! You have now learned everything there is to know about cricket for now. Obviously, all of this may feel a bit overwhelming at first, but now that you've delved into it, you can go ahead and reach for the sky and beyond. Now, go and hit some sixes out of the ground, get some wickets, and take some crazy catches. I truly appreciate it. See ya!

**WORKS CITED**

*https://en.m.wikipedia.org/wiki/History_of_cricket*

*https://en.m.wikipedia.org/wiki/Laws_of_Cricket#:~:text=The%20 earliest%20known%20code%20was,game%20is%20to%20 be%20played.*

*— cite parts from below that you've taken and referenced*

*https://youtu.be/AqtpNkMvj5Y*